Other books by Michael Lieberman:

Praising with My Body

A History of the Sweetness of the World

Sojourn at Elmhurst

Remnant

Far-From-Equilibrium Conditions

Michael Lieberman

Texas Review Press
Huntsville, Texas

FIRST EDITION, 2007

Requests for permission to reproduce material from this work should be sent to:

Permissions
Texas Review Press
English Department
Sam Houston State University
Huntsville, TX 77341-2146

Acknowledgments:

Thanks are due the following journals and anthologies for first printing the following poems, sometimes in slightly different versions:

An Anthology of Texas Poets (Mutabilis Press, 2007. Randall Watson, Editor): "Gratitude," "September 11, 2001."

Houston Poetry Fest, 2005: "Meddling with Parity."

A Summer's Poems (Mutabilis Press, 2006): "Obadiah in Love," "*Trilce Grünbein Mutter Mea.*"

Spiky Palm: "Insufficient Sufis."

Sulphur River Literary Review: "After the First Gulf War."

TimeSlice (Mutabilis Press, 2005. Carolyn Florek, Editor): "Out of Respect for Amedeo Avogadro," "Not for Polish Poets Only"

There are many tests of friendship, and surely one of the most stringent is to read and comment on an unpublished poetry manuscript. Rich Levy, Dan Stern (Oh, how we miss you, Dan), and Adam Zagajewski were kind enough to persevere, their only reward to know that some of the awkwardness has been wrung from this collection. I am also grateful to Paul Ruffin and The Texas Review Press. Paul has been a friend of my poems for many years. Thank you.

Cover photo of painting by Virginia Chévez by Virginia Chévez

Library of Congress Cataloging-in-Publication Data

Lieberman, Michael W., 1941-
   Far-from-equilibrium conditions / Michael Lieberman. -- 1st ed.
      p. cm.
   ISBN-13: 978-1-933896-12-0 (pbk. : alk. paper)
   ISBN-10: 1-933896-12-4 (pbk. : alk. paper)
   I. Title.
   PS3562.I434F37 2007
   811'.54--dc22
                                 2007023708

For Susan, who is at the center of this book and the center of my life
and
for Jonathan and Soyan
and
Seth and Julie

Table of Contents

Gratitude

I

II

III

Far-From-Equilibrium Conditions

Gratitude

I burned the crocuses when they danced naked in gray New Haven—
and after in Pittsburgh and St. Louis. I sat next to no one,
hoarded the oysterettes at my kitchen table in the tired light.
Only once or twice have I allowed myself to teem beyond the ordinary.
And now in this jowled abundance I stumble and dance.
Even if the gloom remain, I am glad for any sun that should rise—
pushed up by her own design or otherwise.
I cling to the tiny strawberries in the wild meadows of certain hearts.
I am the heartworm of those hearts, no more, and I am grateful.

I

Through My Study Window

If a shock of bamboo go
it be silently so
and if it move through me
may its move be slow—
this on days when the wind
says no to stirring willed or wished.

Lied

In my study there is Schubert sitting next to me,
eyeing the schoolyard where Little Franz alone
is singing and the kids are all high fives.
He does not mention that the culture wars consign
him to the fringe, the verge of nothing.
Franz is singing in the choir of himself, not imagining
his voice will break and he will be cast out,
cast in a new role, cast up and away. If today
the songs of Billy Bragg and Wilco or the Pogues are sung
in place of lieder, does it matter to me or the angels
or even Little Franz who is singing in the meadow
of his own imagination? The dust too exults, stirred
by the boys who break dance in the schoolyard now,
just now, and ever in the memory that forgets
Little Franz and his lieder in the schoolyard too.

Meditation on West Gray

Stay with it, I say to myself.
    Get with the program and stay with it.

Li Bai is drunk in a boat on the Yangtze.
    The dam has flooded the river to a stagnant lake.
    Li Bai floats in the current of memory.

Don't go there.
    Stay on West Gray, keep walking.

The marquee of the River Oaks Three is a throw back to the 50's.
    Lots of high-minded films now. Soft focus.
    Hang in there, *El lenguaje del cine es universal.*

I suppose so, like the language of love, like the language of hope,
    like the language of drink, despair . . .
    like Chinese, one text and different sounds.

Go next door, The Epicure serves pastries in three languages—
    consider learning Persian, consider Darius the Great, consider Rumi.
    The language of hunger, the language of conquest, the language of . . .

Paco, my barber, will tell me.
    What's it like, Paco, to grow up gay in Monterrey?
    What's your take on the PRI and Vicente Fox?

Stay on West Gray I repeat to myself.
    Walgreens has it, you can get it there—
    a simple pill for what ails you.

Stop at the dry cleaners—
    he who steals your shirt may steal your soul.
    Consider the soul and neurochemistry—
    Essie has no interest in this delirium,
    she decides to hassle me over my lost ticket.

Modest illumination may accrue along this promenade.
Stay with it, stay on West Gray.

Ignore the sunset, conjecture without fact is an inferno.
Think about Dante, himself an inferno, a score-settler.
Consider learning Italian.

Take instruction.
God knows, take instruction. Horace matters.
Stop at Kroger's, buy a knock-off of a national brand.
Consider a poem, a poem for Dante or Rumi or Horace.
For the moon Li Bai could not embrace.

Insufficient Sufis

Of course they're insufficient,
along with the postal service,
plumbers, doctors, the internet.
Perhaps you were thinking
that because they are holy
or poets or whirl like the wind
when provoked, there would be
something more, a vision,
a levitation, or perfect silence.
Not so. When you get
one of these fellows going
its gab, gab, gab. They drag
out one of the old books,
and let you have it for hours
without end—the world
as they see it. Or answers
to questions no one's asked.
They've never had to deal with merit badges
or an oil change. Try to imagine
a Sufi with a lawnmower. Of course,
they're insufficient for our needs,
they've never been here or done this.
I try to see the world as they see it—
to imagine redemption
beyond the next trash pickup,
salvation beyond direct deposit.
In the blinding sun I want
to expose myself to radiance
and be a little insufficient too.

Longing for Brick and HardiePlank

He noses the plumeria this morning
trying to distinguish among vanillas.
Checks out the stenciled addresses
on the curbs, anchoring himself
to the here of August in Houston,
hoping to provide a permanence
that the shimmering heat
will not carry up and away.
He wants to hug the trash receptacles
to countervail lift with heft,
the ugly ascension
that would force him to dwell
in the fragrance of another world.
He is reassured by contact—
the uneven pavement holds him,
proof of the ordinary imperfection he craves,
now, after angioplasty and stent
have made ascension not a dream,
but a terrible alternative to brick and HardiePlank,
the rain coming through the trees
and striking the windowpanes.

Corbusier and the Research Institute Building

For Doug Hocking, Jay Hoffman, Jill Lerner, Peter Lotz, Jan Maday, Josh Meyer, Kyle Roth, Sid Sanders, Paul Stanaford, Bill Van Horn, & David Watkins

I am the forager of my heart's desire.
Madcap heart, grenadier, what is it you want—
the partitas A. played for you forty years ago,
the bright ribbon in her hair? Walking up the mountain
with Soyan and your son? The erratic flight
of electrons scurrying to be free of night
before it rains? That other man's wife you remember
on the couch in Philadelphia? Dope and drink?
A man looks down on his life as from a hill,
down to a harbor far away and sees the bright tracks
out in the bay as the ships ferry the past to port and beyond—
the passage visible, the passengers too distant.
All the other shes of that life still out of focus.
Go down from that hill, my heart demands,
to the docks, greet the girl from Torrington
you still desire, ask again for other one's partitas.
No, I think, my heart doesn't know its mind.
Take a tough line, strip the sash and saber from grenadier.
Set him down in shirtsleeves with the architects and planners.
Give him his head, let him cast the concrete,
clad the flanks and withers of the building,
the one for mice and fruit flies, the one that must shine
beyond the whiteness of the church in Romchamp,
that must never recede into clarity, the she
who must live in the full, humid presence of Houston.

Out of Respect for Amedeo Avogadro

I swear by Apollo, god of binary decisions
and chemistry, biology & physics
not to divulge the value of Avogadro's number
or how it is calculated to anyone
who has not taken high school chemistry.
I will never speak with poets about Apollo and Dionysus
or the role of yeast in bread and wine.
I will not discuss transubstantiation.
If someone should come knocking saying speak,
I will offer cinnabar of mercury and sulfur and retreat.
In a corner of my youth the ideal gas law sleeps—
R, a constant reminder of what connects the forces of the world.

Conjecture

The future has no moving parts.
Schools of engineering will crease to exist,
docents will shred all evidence of pistons,
longing will hiss into space through a frozen valve.
Someone will silence song,
middle C will be a trace on a screen,
microcircuits will be unnecessary,
music will hemorrhage and die.
The heart's lub-dub will dwindle,
tenderness will persist in binary code,
love will vibrate like atoms in the gruel of space,
we will wonder why song existed,
kisses will be a remembered fiction,
touch will be something that was.
The torque of nothingness will ratchet us down.

The Crux of the Matter

Went out in the darkness, looked for the paper.
Not yet. No leaves in the elms. No leaves
on the crape myrtle either. Hibiscus buds.
Logged on to CNN.com. No news. El País reports
a roof collapse in Poland, sixty dead, others injured.
Like a giant black lily the world opens—
oblivious to its self as blossom, an orange blossom.
The marvelous circumstance of being, of being
unfurled as the flower opens even without the dawn.

Lucca

Take the train from Pisa—
the boy across the aisle
complains to a cell phone
about a failed romance,

slogans in spray paint
demand obedience
from abandoned stations,

a mutilated stump
of sycamore moans,
wisteria lurch in the wind,

Lucca is cinnabar and mustard,
houses that crimp the ancient
amphitheater, treeless,
trying to imagine spring,

just at the edge of the moat
a god whipsaws a sheet of tin
to announce the rain,

somewhere a physicist
is stirring his bosons and quarks,
waiters are setting out glasses,

in dimpled siestas
the gnocchi dream of the forces
that hold the spring together.

Chutney

My conjecture is paltry, no more than this:
The Master of the Universe has given
Major Grey a special dispensation

with regard to order. Now he lurks
hidden in the heraldry, the pomp,
the foliage that always befuddles me

on the same shelf of every Kroger's,
an obscure aristocrat, unflappable,
slipped into a socket next to teriyaki glaze

across the aisle and down from jam.
Perhaps this placement is a glimmer
of free will among the marketers

or the *carpe diem* of the planners,
or just the random strike of chance events.
Once he lived free among the maharajas,

now he is prisoner of our restricted selves.
What of the shopkeeper Mr. Poonjiaji, his spicy
informant? And Gray? Does he sit on a decrepit throne?

What obsolescence does he occupy?
What does any of us merit who sets one stone,
one pebble, on another in the dark

or hears the chiaroscuro chant of birds,
thinks tumescent thoughts, and lunges
after stock on the sundry shelves of the mind?

At a New England Pond

after García Lorca

I sat down
in a space
outside of time
copper beech lake pine
and stuttered
trying to break the shell
excluding me

My son sat down
outside in my space of time
trying to include me
and I left behind
beech and lake and pine

I sat looking
for the motive
behind the look
when all there is
is beech and lake and pine

What played upon
time's mind that day
also played on mine
excluded all
but beech and lake and pine.

Waiting for You at Lake Morena

For Zachary Andrew Wingman Lieberman (b. Aug 23, 2007)

The cottonwoods cling bitterly to the alkali at Lake Morena
and I wait for you.

There are miners trapped in Utah and an earthquake in Peru
and I wait for you.

Six-hundred die in floods in North Korea and others here
and I wait for you.

Not that you can redistribute forces, change the tides, or raise the dead
but I wait for you.

You will not reverse offenses we have given to this planet
but I wait for you.

I wait for your debut, instructor of the flawed heart—and flawed as well
yet you must do.

And still the cottonwoods cling bitterly to the alkali at Lake Morena
and I wait for you.

You will not move them to oak and hickory and then to beech
that is too much for you to do.

Yet I wait, little gurgler, giver of life, alien voyager from within us,
I wait for you to do — and do and do.

To José Chávez Morado

the painter, who was born near Guanajuato in 1904 (according to one
version and 1909 in another) and was featured in the culture section
of a Mexico City daily (April 11, 2001) (where I first encountered him)
because he is giving more of his library and papers to the public,
who at 97 is confined to a wheelchair and, although a one-time communist,
looks very prosperous in his conservative tie and white shirt, and is an admirer
of Lázaro Cárdenas, who nationalized big oil, and whose works
are everywhere in every style in Mexico and the Phoenix Museum of Art—
I want you to know how much I love the reproduction of "Carnaval de
Huejotzino" in the paper (which I also found, along with a painting of
Guanajuato, on the net), the raw confrontation of a bandit with death is
sincere whimsy, sacred camp in your country's long struggle. But you died
before I could deliver my little homage, my *homenajito*. I am buoyed
by what you have lofted—you hoisted stratospheric the payload
of your country's soul, like an incandescent second-stage Diego, and gave
presence to what is present only in its absence, raconteur of dark forces.

Messenger RNA

What do we do with a drunken sailor,
the little fella at the bar who says
watch out for your genome, the poisonous
glitches that spell doom in your forties
or death in your fifties? Give him
another drink and he'll talk gibberish,
sober him up and he'll have you
on a high fiber diet. No sense in piping
up the band, he's bleary-eyed, no chance
he's going to dance or tell you more.
No wonder he's drinking in the bar,
he's been sent to deliver a message
that won't be well received. Spare us,
bounce this treacherous Phaedippas
before he tells us more.

Port of Call

Freighted with antiquities
and crates of modern work
the Menil steams into our lives
glad tidings in its wake.
From its deck Magritte
is calling our name.

The Otherness

I wage a savage fight against insomnia,
even as I struggle to salvage the night,
to dive down beneath the darkness
and haul the unseen to the surface.
I listen to the hollow blow of a train
headed south across San Filipe.
Someone's mouser screeches at its prey.
The dog next door yaps blindly at another,
his point not altogether clear.
This ordinary tryst distracts me until
supplanted by another—a truck, its engine
straining to lift a dumpster from a parking lot,
a clanking virtue in the December chill.
More. Tire-squeal along West Gray,
the raucous snort of a drunk.
Another blow, the forced hot air
of the furnace obliterates this world.
I listen for some clue
while hibiscus roots push into resistant clay,
our neighbor's Chinese elm sheds
its leaves into my awareness, my wife
sleeps in a good marriage. I strain to hear
this world, the one that burgeons
with sounds unheard, unknown, unheeded.

Meddling with Parity

True law is right reason in agreement with nature.
Cicero

Physicists sweet-talk common sense to death
and leave us with our jigsaw lives
to make the world whole again.
Without regard to need—
the Lord's or ours—
they've overthrown parity,
cut the last best hope free of mind,
and turned us to blind faith.
My argument went:
Dear Lord, we thank You
for order in a universe of chaos—
for miracles like atoms, cells,
development, the Coriolis effect,
the gift of language, especially,
the tower of Babel, *und so weiter.*
The devil was entropy
and Your gift a structured universe.
Lee and Yang are meddlers of the worst type,
infidels who set the dogs on order,
cornered You in a gritty taqueria,
and beat the tar out of Your right reason.
So, this morning when I look
at the sea and find the line between the sky
and water shrouded to oblivion,
I understand how meaningless
distinctions are to You
and thus to me—which, as You have willed,
supports the overthrow of parity.
Lord, you are stingy in revealing your intentions.

II

Penelope, the Woman

She sits alone at the kitchen table waiting.
This time he does not return. She doesn't know why.
Perhaps he has AIDS or Alzheimer's, has found
another woman. Maybe he lost a leg to diabetes.
She only knows that he has not returned.
She pours herself a cup of tea and wonders
if he will call. She writes a check to the gas company,
tries not to think about him in her rent-controlled apartment.

Foreplay

Then there was the other one,
the one interested in Kierkegaard
who would solemnly engage me.
I didn't know a thing about Kierkegaard
and so I would parry with John Stuart Mill,
hoping that would move love along.
Which it didn't.

Instruction

Three things, he said, a man should do
before he dies—see *The Magic Flute*,
savior an artichoke, make love to a beautiful woman.
Still I am not ready. The poets of the Tang Dynasty,
what about them—those thousands whom
we barely remember? Was it enough to drink
rice wine and make love under the thunderheads?

Hardwired

Sometimes love can reign in desire
as when he looks across the room
at the stunning young woman
in the sheath and thinks,
'What am I thinking?'
And sometimes it can't.
Some clarity would help.

A Woman

After trimming a stubborn bougainvillea
that hardly flowered in the heat,
I remember Ahkmatova's revelation
that she could neither accept nor reject
her suitor Nedobrovo.

Weather

for Susan

There is a snapshot,
    taken I think at Whittemore,
        in Saint Louis, the occasion

David and Brenda's wedding
    from which you are absent—
        your mother,

younger than we are now,
    looks out next to me
        and to the side are both

our boys, almost toddlers.
    What would your absence
        be like?

The only thing I remember
    distinctly from that day
        is flowers

not the wedding bouquet
    or those arranged on the tables,
        but catalpa

in the back yard blooming —
    big and generous clusters,
        the delicacy of each

lost in the massing of the whole.
    So much like you
        (how unsuited is the rose).

In Houston, flowers
    even in robustness
        are not facsimile of you.

It is the weather
    I need.
        The splendid turbulence

that tumbles out of
    thirty thousand feet
        in dark festoons and pours

the contents of the world
    on top of us.
        Which is not

to dwell on the darkness
    in you, but to say
        the force of your love

is natural and grand
    and finds its way down to earth.
        The intimidating rains

of these clouds nourish all flowers
    that grow here,
        that survive the weather's onslaught.

There is a danger in this power,
    but you have
        managed to control it.

The weather
    is disorienting here.
        No winter to speak of,

and many years
    the spring is summer, and summer
        an infernal time

when the metabolism withers,
    cicadas quite early
        and one hibernates till fall.

Fall is confounding
    for its mildness that predicts
        a colder phase in which

some flowers prosper,
    but is not by any stretch
        a summer.

I can't compare thee
    to a summer's day,
        they don't exist in Houston.

I must choose particulate weather
    like thunderheads to engage
        your passion

that feels to me
    colossal.
        And torrential rains,

here as fierce as anything
    in the tropics,
        that expose the seams of the land,

then give way to mildness.
    How else but weather
        to capture you? The generosity

that rain brings to the soil—
> rain that
>> rejuvenates the sea—

not its erosive power
> but what fills us
>> down to our last cell.

Whatever dryness
> is in me, you have
>> washed out to sea.

Look at any weather map—
> at the isotherms and isobars,
>> those lines of constant

temperature and pressure, and you
> will believe we understand
>> squalls and hurricanes,

that the scientist's imagination
> has put to rest
>> the randomness of process,

that chaos theory has no role,
> that everything is in order.
>> That's how a meteorologist,

would see it—
> all causes may
>> be understood by rational analysis.

Yet we know such maps
> are fictions, at best approximations,
>> that no one, at least

not now, can predict
        what moisture off the Gulf
                will do when it collides

with cool air moving south.
        I concede that in a general way
                we know we're in for rain.

But isn't it like a kiss?—there are
        kisses and then there are kisses.
                So one can never tell

about the rain in Houston.
        We know
                every so often there will be

a hurricane or something worse,
        a storm with a benign name
                like Allison that will

stagger us. That's the joy
        in your love—you never fail
                to stagger me, your kisses

blow off the sea with a strength
        and subtlety that leave
                the weather wanting.

No man has a right
        to so much. (I know that
                few men have it).

Anyone with a kite
        and patience can draw
                lightning from the sky.

But how many have a shot
     at our electrifying joy
          when we make love?

We know with precision
     how one air mass
          rubs against another

to transfer electrons
     to create capacitance and discharge
          and make sparks fly.

But how is it that
     you and I
          lacking every instrument

have the means
     to incinerate the sky
          and leave it blue?

How is it that in perfect weather
     this act plays out
          as love and not release?

This chemistry is still a mystery,
     of course we know
          about tactility,

afferent neurons to the brain,
     the rush of hormones,
          but these explanations

of human lightning
     leave us cold
          and humdrum.

You've made a marriage
   of explaining this to me
      who often gets it wrong.

If I'm condemned
   to be your student always,
      well, good that I fancy the teacher.

The humidity of September
   is a postscript
      a coda whose ink

is smeared by the heat
   as it tries to reach
      out into the midst

of us, into the hugeness
   of our love
      and swamp it, as the sea

might overwhelm fish
   mollusk, crustacean, kelp
      and cede to plankton.

Hard to think,
   my love, that our love
      is plankton love,

the moving loam
   of the sea
      its landless soil

churned by the wind, exposed,
   common, abundant
      and uniquely ours.

Encounter

He would take the phone from her politely.
Once or twice we talked about Pound, sometimes Dante,
but mostly he thanked me for helping her,
as if this were Thira and the great wound
of the caldera had to be closed, forgetting
how he healed me, how self-serving Dante was.

Modesty

Desire is falling in great fat flakes,
especially in America, especially in the movies
in New Haven in the sixties and later
in her car where we did all manner of things,
then dry humped until I was raw. You see,
she wanted to remain a virgin.

Younger Man, Older Woman

Then there was Juan,
poor Juanito, moony
over Rosita and her brood.
At sixteen in high school,
he felt himself lucky
to come home to her
each afternoon.
He would do anything
to marry her—mop floors,
sell dope, drop out of school.
He was as smitten with her
as Bolivia with coca.
Anything, he thought, anything.
Poor Juanito, he was suicidal
when she threw him out, a kid
with no money, no green card.
His life was over.
What bad luck, what good luck.

Trying to Get It Right

A man looks at a young woman
then past her at a giant cooper beech
trying to imagine how the Lord
managed to get it right with them,
why He refused to do so with the others,
why He taunts us with imperfection,
why it matters when there are
irises, strong coffee and the wind.
She is unimportant, the man insists,
knowing he cannot give up the lie.

Obadiah in Love

Obadiah took a stab at prophecy—
just a snippet wedged among the others,
five minutes of predicting doom. Nothing more.
Did he dismiss this voice in favor of the world?
He might have farmed or traded dates and raisins,
a middle man, perhaps a trafficker, a profiteer.
Did he find love with his wife or was he an ally cat
or gay or lacking in desire? Can a prophet cheat
in love? What do prophets do when madness
dies and they are free of visions? Buy tangerines
from vendors in the streets, umbrellas? Could he
imagine grace or how sex might ripen into love?

III

Translational Energy

All morning I thrashed about
trying to find a way in
when what I wanted
was to tumble out,
a molecule thrumming
beyond allowed transitions.

Leaving Pittsburgh

I've been leaving every day
for forty years—the streetcars,
Panther Hollow, Roy Jones' lips
cracked from playing trumpet,
the day school that doused me
with chemistry and set me afire,
its hymnal, Latin, teen-age breasts.
I'm leaving Pittsburgh, headed out,
everything I own in the back seat,
leaving what's absent, what sits
on the cracked curbs, the acrid air
clutching at me, the midden of Pittsburgh
the ailanthus trees and locusts,
the infernal gray of the sky,
the rose climbing cream-colored
against the kitchen window,
lilacs, my skin,
I'm leaving Pittsburgh intact,
never leaving it behind.

The Jack Man

At Keystone Box, Herbie
worked the pump jack,
a long-armed, levered hydraulic
that hoisted skids and pallets
he'd drag off to trucks
bound for Brockway Grass
or Ford City's bottling plant.
His job was to keep up,
keep the skids a coming,
and the workers humming,
not to let the line slow,
since this was piece work,
and they were bonused by the speed
they fed the cardboard in
and he swept the bundled cartons
truckward to the loading dock.

He wedged a wad between his gum
and cheek. Silence. No word passed
between him and the others. Wild-eyed,
he leaned on the long-stemmed handle
that once had claimed Don Wrobel's
teeth when something slipped
and it whipped through its arc.
The only flick of life was Herbie's
Adam's apple. He waited for a crew
to top off a load and motion him.

Don't think of the grit of Pittsburgh
or the lives as gray as the days.
Try to imagine the Serengeti,
Herbie haunched at the ready
eyeing the hyenas that fed him,
the lionesses that serviced him,

or a man in a denim shirt and jeans
on furlough from Western Psych
with a fistful of pills and knuckles
so clenched he could not take them.
May God preserve him—and all
the hapless jack men moving
this world forward on its skids.

Coaxing the Muse

Sometimes she is arthritic and could use
a boost, a tonic, something to get the juices going.
I've seen muses get stubborn, sulk in a corner
and refuse to help. They toss their sultry locks
and give you that get-stuffed-buddy look.
Just when you're ready to pickup your bag
and head for the park—you've got the idea
you'll watch a game of chess and write a bit—
she gives you that tough-broad look, digs in her heels
and says she aches and wants to stop for tea.

It's not supposed to work this way I tell her.
You're my muse, you've got obligations.
Inspiration's hard work. Get with the program.
Get real. I can see I'm having no effect.
Before I turn muse-beater, I gig her—
if you think you want another job,
you're going to need a reference.
If you don't get off your fat you-know-what
and help, I don't know what I'm going to write.
She levels her eyes at me as if to say: I'm tired,
I'm not sure I want to work much longer,
I've got some money socked away, and what
with social security and all, I'll manage.
Besides, musing's work for younger chicks.

Mechanical Bird

The vent on my neighbor's roof
flutters through the pepper tree
like an unnamable bird, part of
a menagerie trapped in my view
through the window. What does
it mean to trap the unnamable
as a trophy for the heart's aviary,
when the heart is shrunken
in retreat in the chest? A relic
dropped in place by a contractor
is all that binds me to the fabricated
songbirds of my world.
I should call my sons in Boston,
ask them about continuance,
if they've sighted something similar
this morning. They know about
continuance, about building.
Has something similar happened
to them on the other coast?
Rakish dancer beyond my tree,
no change of light will send
you south this winter. You are
as captive as my heart, jailed
by a rib cage that keeps trying
to expand. On my neighbor's
roof you are ensnared by flashing.
You thrash, you cannot fly up
to the lushness of the world.

Trilce Grünbein Mutter Mea

Chaste mother, unfunky mother, survivor,
your father Stutz-Bear-Catted thruuuu
the roaring twenties, chased the girls
and loved the ponies. Your birthright,
Rita Lee, was Hobart Street (its daffodils
befuddled you), a mother your husband
called miNerva, and the white gloves
she brought from Lynchburg.
Fragile as porcelain, you survived uncracked
to raise me—me, the milk groveler,
little circumcised me, the lettuce-couraged warrior.
Your mother bound your feet and left you
a larva, a neotenic salamander mother.
Stream dweller, you are the proper dead woman
who raised me in the chards of your own survival.
I of the shattered vessel, fractured
beyond leaky. It is said (though
who can believe it?) that on the last day
of the world Christ will raise the dead.
I have assigned you to that file drawer.
I, your untender son (the physician), let lava rains
destroy a love that in the end was only
sulcus deep. The showered emboli diminished me,
not you, late vase-ensnarer of daffodils.

The Earth is Preparing Me

This should be a scene in which
I am in a forest of conifer and birch,
lichens facing north on the pitted stones.
I should be sitting there taking stock
on this the anniversary of my father's birth,
wondering about the earnest movement
of the beetles on a rotting log, if their clamber
can signify anything beyond the inevitable.
I should be preparing for the time
the log is carbon dioxide and water,
but I'm scrunched on a bench in Houston,
stifled by the heat of September,
looking at the uniformity of the cars,
it's hard to tell each passing from the next.
I try to imagine the merits of this bench,
the street, the city, my life as it nears its end.
This much is certain: I will be absorbed
into the cacophonous roar of being
and deaf grace will be indifferent.

Karl Shapiro

You called Da Ponte Mozart's Jew,
but he was yours as well.
Exiled, you lived free in verse,
a free-shooter, a libertine
who fondled every text and held none sacred,
unless by sacred we mean shining
and then there were many. Omnivore,
Ovid and Whitman served you equally.
You shredded the rulebook, torched
the confetti, and took a buzz saw to civility.
They exiled you, but your poetry survived.
When they lashed your coffin
to a flatbed and shipped you to the prairies,
you drilled an air hole with your awl
and bellowed out your lines. You were
an American Zeus lifting the skirts
of Europa in the alien corn and silage.
Jew, edgy kike, my kike,
let these lines stand as Kaddish
for you, a poet, who still lives free.

Advent

He did not come
a wild radiance
from the bayous
a glistening apparition
from beneath
the elevated highway
armed with knowing vapors
gleaming.

He has been
sitting here
dilapidated
as the patio of Café Brazil
drinking tea
from a mug
in the company of students
ruminating
on what message
they expect beyond
"I greet you
from the ordinary."

If tonight
a shabby moon shine
through the agnostic air
it is an act
defying physics
that abandons him
and burns through
this unholy poem
that chooses
at this moment
to abandon luminosity

and offer
bottled lemon
for the tea
a plastic spoon.

The Day of the Poem in the Papers

[N]ovela y reportaje son hijos de una misma madre.
Gabriel García Márquez

Pictures of people standing in front of pictures of Auschwitz
on the anniversary of its liberation. The gothic script
of the masthead reminds you that we speak their language.
You zip your windbreaker trying to insulate yourself,
unable to remember what you've been freed of.

The man-eating crocs in Malawi are devouring
the villagers because the rivers are over-fished.
The government should restock the rivers.
Presto, just like that. They really should restock.
I suddenly remember my car-door opener needs a battery.

One *caudillo* savages another at a press conference.
A *rueda de prensa*, literally the wheel of the press.
The rack of the press is always better than the press of events.
I think of Richard Dreyfuss in *Moon Over Parador*.

Yesterday, according to the paper, was the deadliest day
of the war in Iraq—no, that day comes
when Congress cuts Medicaid to pay for Humvees.
Why does the dog of politics gnaw the bone of decency?

A futurist takes our palm in his, predicts how many
of us will floss tomorrow, surely this is
more important than toting up the dead.

Dante was not political, Thomas à Beckett was only pious,
Hammarskjöld was a seeker. At all costs avoid seekers,
law and order demands it. We sleep under a down quilt,
dreaming, imagining that soldiers of fortune will save us.

It is January in Houston, get ready for red bud,
remember, you swim outdoors all year here.
Put deficits and poverty on the shelf—
alphabetized for easy access:
Beckett, Dante, Deficits, Hammarskjöld, Medicaid, Poverty.

Which of these is about agribusiness, the toxic stench
of manure from the hog farms in the Midwest? Its map is
a quilt of American values cut and sewn from our dopey dreams.

Release will come when you are paroled from grace
to enter into the world of the living dumpster.
You listen to the clarinet concerto. It is Mozart's birthday.

September 10, 2001

for Linda Gregg and Jack Gilbert

The day tilts like Falling Water
slipping toward the falls on Bear Run.
Hemlock and mountain laurel, unaware,
suck moisture from the hills.
Jack might have said, 'Not that way,
that's not what I remember.'
Time measures our world, never buying
fabric for the suit it cannot wear.
It cannot hold its lover in its arms.
The world is not without end.
When they arrived on Monolethos
the trace of the catastrophe was evident,
the caldera hacked from the island
and the pumice on the beaches.
It was like Eden the day after the fall.
The day before had been her birthday,
but it seemed only a matter of hours
since the angry thrust of molten lava
did away with love and then civility.
A radiance shown off the sea,
a mist rolling in each day obscured
why they came. It ended the way
the mills in Pittsburgh ended—
with corrosion seeping into the girders
and implosion. We are sojourners
in our own land. We pray for peace.
We row toward restoration in the swells,
only a few poems to show for our efforts,
not our superhuman efforts,
but the human ones flourishing in detail.

September 11, 2001

1. Kyrie

This is the same porch I sat on reading Mihail Sebastian,
    where I drank the same double strength coffee
    and brooded,
the same place where I wondered about apologists for evil
    and those who brook no apology for evil,
where today I am confronting secrets, meanings I imagine—
    a dog circling before the hearth or lifting its leg
    to a tree, acts that are not predestined but inevitable,
necessary for the business of being a dog, how our
    behavior is nourished by the cells we nourish,
    and the flowers on every stem are both different
    and the same.
For some events awkward anapests pretend root causes,
    yet what seems encrypted in culture resides
    a layer down.
So when I look at the encumbering dactyls of the past
    that clasp us, I move to the realm of spiders and
    insects, how they engulf or burrow into their mates
    and prey—
as if Fabre, not Clausowitz, explained Bunker Hill and
    Dien Bien Phu, as if the how-to of solitary wasps
    is our guide.
The boiler-plate evil of the twentieth century remains
    with us, not a repeat of the past, but a portrayal
    of the tumbling shards of our neural circuits.

God is relative and a relative, holding forth at the podium
    on sundry items—the shrink-wrapped odds and
    ends of our lives—
all talk is sundry and relative. My God does not trash,
    He's not a gossip, but when He represents His
    views, there's no correspondence,
nothing lingers but indefinable essences that find no place
    in words—the smell of basil and the smell of shit.

When I read of Mihail Sebastian reproving the evil -escu's
    of his world and how dactylic Homer left Achilles
    dead, I cannot not grasp the meaning or rely on
    grief and pity.
The Iron Guard in Romania is a play with too many
    characters, and our legacy of Troy remains small
    towns, football teams and condoms.
Our world is a map without coordinates, ditto our
    ministrations to the Lord. What are good works
    good for? We cannot apply a yardstick to a song.
Try to imagine a croissant without olfaction, a club
    without prehension, chess without cognition.
    Try to imagine God Almighty.

The subbasement of the Towers is amines and serotonin,
    receptors and evolution, developmental biology
    and animal behavior.
I long for relativism that is relevant. Whether there is one
    God or not I do not know, but there are many
    prophets—Darwin, Lorenz, Tinbergen, Von
    Frisch, E.O. Wilson, others.
In Provence Van Gogh and Gauguin grappled to find a
    way in by looking out. For Vincent the merge
    of sun and wheat and sky yielded the essential
    truth of chartreuse, a gaudy remnant that Gauguin
    refused in his own distortions, the two of them
    struggling in Arles, working in Vincent's yellow
    house.
And Others. Pasteur in Paris dissected the inner logic of
    chirality in lactic acid crystals and Emil Fischer
    concurred, Mahler and Bruckner embraced music
    to expel their demons, Freud and Jung like two
    hemispheres of thought forced us bolt-upright
    in the night,
Pairs of fraternal twins, towering above their peers
    divergent and convergent, resistant to implosion,
    fanatic and committed.

2. Gloria

Dear Wystan Hugh,
I wish I had your view
(or what was thought your view)
of love and death.
What's up my sorcerer sleeve
is that there's no reprieve.
Nothing ends with whimper or sigh—
we won't love one another, but die.

Each reads his sacred text,
no better than the next,
to secure a hearth and home,
permission for a bomb.
We're right, of course we're right
except when we are wrong.
Our offenses are less egregious
simply because we're religious,
our humanists agree—
they're us without a trinity.

3. Credo

When it comes to rubble and loss,
I believe in nostalgia—speak-easys
and gangsters with tommy guns,
the rags-to-riches ketch that spares us.
What obscures skewers —
the pipes of Hibernians
marching on St. Patrick's Day
mean homage and resolve.
No script or text takes precedence,
no pretext can prevail—
pre-text impulses flood our every action.
Impulse is what gives impulse traction.

Our inheritance is neurons.
Being well connected means our axons.
Memory is triplet snags of DNA
that catch our decency and dreams
as schemes for tomorrow and today.
We struggle with these, against these,
improvident beings whose search
for the light consists only of sight.
Our retinas and cortical patterns
capture the surface of what happens—
spelling bees, saints and slatterns,
Jihad, Koran, and Talibans—
valued by mindless acts of mind.

We live with loss and reprisal
turning over in our minds,
a zero-sum game, a sudden-death match
with every knight and pawn both black and white.
From every shires ende
to happenstance we *wende*.
No contortion helps us slip our bind.
No destiny is manifest,
our only hope is kindness met in kind.

September 11, 2002, Meditation

I am watching a rerun of events at ground zero on Univisión—
self-improvement is such a relentless American pastime.
I struggle to keep up with death extruded from the craw
of a second language, the distance granting permission.
A young Hispanic mother, pregnant with twins
when her husband burned, is saying something beyond language,
something I cannot understand.
                              My ten-minute drive
to work takes thirty—a man is trimming dead blossoms
from his mandevilla, a harvest for life, I think. I stop
to write this down and remember a friend's poem
I gave my wife this morning, one about a single, homeless
woman celebrated there. I measure this
against three thousand, the lottery of premeditated evil
that helps us measure loss.
                          A minute later I am driving,
put on notice—*los corridos* banished—by a moment of silence
on Hispanic radio at the instant the first plane hit the Tower.
I'm stopped again wondering what happiness I should pause to remember
or put aside in remembrance, what abundance or good fortune?—
being born white and Jewish in Pittsburgh, not brown in Michoacán,
no hope for them beyond survival in the shadowy game of morning here.
How shabbily we treat our many selves—some days you can buy
Mexican limes at 20 for a dollar. Revealed truth is everywhere
in the scrub of Texas.
                      What would we put on a National Identity Card?—
something repulsive like 'this migrant picker wanted
to be a software engineer,' or 'this software engineer wanted
to be a martyr.' It is certain we need quotas, we have abundant
martyrs. The homeowner is still trimming death
from his flowers.

After the First Gulf War

The tubers extrude their irises—
a blur of impertinence at my front door—
and spring molts to the boil of summer.

My sister ices her knees in St. Louis
and sings the white-girl marathon blues.
The Sumerians do not bolt from their sleep.

There is so much downtime waiting
for history in the desert or watching
the goldsmiths on the Ponte Vecchio.

I stay at home, but once I ventured out
and almost like finding a sphinx in the desert,
I came across triumphant Jagiello

in the snow of Central Park. I do not know
how these transportations begin across
the energy barrier of what's reasonable.

The camera is history's gin—we don't
want to see the vassals plotting or
a has-been king conniving. Take us, we

demand, direct to Runnymede for the signing.
Unknown thousands of Iraqis dead in the desert,
our men at rest in battle dress and dervish turrets—

not once in Iraq did a hero pull a sword from a forge.
I want a voiceover, something authoritative
or holy to settle like a cloud in place

of the shroud of talk eroding our dead.
What swarms is anomie of the heart,

a storm of despair that drives
the orphan in me to the open—in that glade
the blue bullets burst into flower
and force me to resign my gambit.

After they hammer metal into ornaments,
what do they do, where do they go,
the goldsmiths from the Ponte Vecchio?

Do they go for broke—a pizza and a coke,
surf the channels for the soccer scores,
news of other wars, a renegade John Wayne?

Where do I go, vagrant on the bayou—
open a tin and wait for the cockroach thrum
to drown out the all-defeating echoes of Pittsburgh?

Tsunami

December, 2004

It's 6 am near the corner of Draper and Pearl.
Café Milano creaks with the rock of the sea,
tosses and turns, dreams a dream of plenty.
In its happiness, it longs for nothing—
not porsciutto, nor pecorino, not osco bucco.
It raises no glass of Asti Spumante.
It has not interest in tiramisu,
it slumbers without a shudder,
not even dreaming of the wake
rising beyond the Pacific rim.

Navicular

January, 2005

The small bones of the hand
are an archipelago of fear
that grasp at the splintered wood
as it slips between the fingers.
Beneath the sea is sinew,
molten beyond our ken. Above it
indifferent gulls lunge at the arcs
of fish who care nothing for sulfur or pumice.
Beyond the torso of Asia
the krill that crest with the waves
ignore our white-knuckle lives,
spill with the churn of the sea
to be swallowed by their own cetacean world.
From the shoals of our routine
gratitude erupts in slow motion.
We find a pen, write a check,
put the kettle on to boil,
make a cup of tea,
and sit at the kitchen table,
thankful for taxes and partisan bickering.

Esplanade

We walk from the Cove
    along the coast
        toward Draper St.
Hard sun
    smacking the sea
        into submission, almost
lush but no sanctuary,
    resistant in the extreme.
        Six dollar straw hat
from Von's
    protecting what's nascent in me
        from relentlessness.
Hot for La Jolla
    not for everywhere
        not for the Sonora Desert
not for Paris, there,
    the worst heat wave
        ever registered.
The runners are walking here,
    they are walking
        in Tulsa too.
Sea appeases
    sky's appetite
        for moisture.
No one gets out
    of paradise alive.
        If they ascend
they are wicked away
    like mist
        off the sea—to where?
or sucked and sluiced
    like kelp
        borne south

with the current.
    Beauty drains us
        (even beauty)
even in cheap straw hats
    even when quenched by diet Pepsis—
        resistance is drawn
out of us
    like water
        from the furrows
of the sea
    up and away from the Pacific
        up and away from paradise.

Gloss

Chilean Spring

Santiago—Saint Iago—
Fire in the branches
of the cherry trees.
Wet grass under my feet.

The North

Antofagasta, dry as a liar's mouth.
Calama whispers nothing.
San Pedro de Atacama,
sultan's eunuch, guards
the Valley of the Moon—
grit and bone.

The South

that austral courtesan—
slick as an ad for trout
in an outdoor magazine.

Isla Negra

Neruda wrote a patter song with his life in this house—
the rooms are filled with shells, maidenheads, butterflies
and moths, mounted beetles and cockroaches, African masks
(we're told he never visited, gifts from friends), a trophy stove,
a bust of Jenny Lind, a papier maché horse from childhood,
a spyglass, writing desks (four, one made from the driftwood
door of a ship's cabin), a bed where he and Matilde slept,
pictures of Baudelaire, Whitman, Poe, Balzac, García Lorca,
Whitman again, closets with his clothes, memorabilia
from Burma, Ceylon, Jakarta, samples of his hand writing.
The table is set, a chair marked with a signifying place mat
for the captain of this Pacific trader, this silent house,
chockablock with everything but words. Out a window
beyond his grave, the sea in three-quarters view,
a cowlick of waves around the black rocks in the breakers.

String Theory

About one's dispatch there is no informed consent.
I will be assigned as nothing.
May it be a significant nothing,
a nothing to be proud of—
the leaf stripped clean to its veins
or just the mandible-hoisted green itself
or its chlorophyll, stomach-cleared,
enzyme-sheared to molecules,
the bleary wavelets of our universe
adrift in a universe of universes.

Andersen Double Hung Windows

1.

October wind off the Charles, gray sky overtaking the skullers,
and in the Harvard COOP I buy *A Defense of Ardor*,
lie around the attic bedroom of my son's house
and implore its heat to redeem the impatiens from the frost.
Even the Heights of Macchu Picchu can bring one to despair.

Call out the gods, I say, let them preserve
the tulip bulbs and geese on Jamaica pond.
Select one to be Nameless and organize a universe (ours, Lord)
as an example to chaos, a wager to entropy.
Invest him with body and gender. Let him reign
over sinks, cathedrals, caterwauls, catharsis.

I prop myself up on an elbow, eyelevel with the starlings
and worry over coffee, children (mine), their wives,
my wife, and not the willful evil of our age—
a compendium of indecencies that has no meaning,
a dishonor roll of evil. I ignore the particular.

Unnamable Majesty, how can you hear my prayers
when you too are deaf to detail, when I cannot speak,
when you live in a vacuum beyond my universe
where sound waves cannot travel?
Or do I have it backwards—I live in a vacuum
that is beyond your universe and praise cannot exit?

2.

The windows of my son's house have counterweights
of a kind not used today, the smooth glide
of wood on metal belies the cracking sills.

So when the furnace bangs and I swelter,
it is a breeze to lift the frame, remove my sweater,
let in the dank of Boston, the vapors off
the shriveled plants, and stoke what ardor's
given me, what's lost and necessary,
what's promised by mulch and mold,
the solitary bud on next spring's rhododendron.

3.

I write to praise liberated shopping carts,
and especially one, whose owner I think is R.
who is eighty with a touch of sugar and a spirit
larger than the sky. She needs that cart.
I need her buoyancy. Once I was scarred
by righteous indignation over vagrant
shopping carts—I think back to when I was
my son's age and reading Fanon's
The Wretched of the Earth without sympathy.
I have no idea if Andersen double-hung windows
exist in Algeria or why I rejected every word.
Today his concern curls over my son's chimney,
his rightness marred by anger, his vision
dimmed by the blinding Saharan sun.

Egon Schiele at the Neue Galerie

Eros marked his body with her own —
arms, thighs, bone, eyes, breasts, cunt.
He struggles, clasped in her beak,
squeezed unsparingly by her demands,
pumping color from the sky and trees,
flaying his body so that we can see.
This demand, this dare, asks
that we abandon home and family,
strike out on the road to immolation.
He offers us no choice — examine
every crease, every labial hair.
If love demand a wretched death,
I pick a luncheonette on a deserted avenue.
Let my last meal be ham on rye and fries.
In the name of what is spare and unholy,
extreme brother, I bear your mark —
and hers — bear it as much as I dare.
I ask that some impure flame consume me,
that you fold this prayer and place it
in the wall between the stones.

Not for Polish Poets Only

1.

For now, goodbye to Krakow
and the instruments of Canon Copernik,
the astrolabium from Cordova and the sextant of doubt.
Goodbye, rectors in your robes
and poets watering geraniums and waiting for a sign,
pigeons on the square, goodbye —
any biology student can inform on you.
Goodbye to Saint Mary's and your discarded leaflets
and to the bugler explained therein,
to good King Jagiello who continues
at this very moment to prevail against the Teutons
and the little restaurant behind him
where we ate pirogues and drank beer.

Goodbye to the phlox, hydrangea and willows —
sentries on the road to Auschwitz, a set with no actors.
We need a read through of what happened,
a handful of violets for each speaker at the end.
Goodbye to those events that never happened,
much more distant than Grunwald.
Jagiello lives, Copernik struggles, the rain
dissolves the face of the stones in the square.

2.

The oldest square in Central Europe
was revived 1989. I do a little foxtrot there,
a shuffle for the uncertainty of progress,
the net, the fax and email. I hover over coffee
listening for microwaves, scanning the infrared
for a sign, expecting a message in regal ultraviolet.

At this moment not even ouzo could make me snake
between the tables in praise of Aphrodite.

I forgive those who carved the Jew musicians in the Cloth Hall —
after all, a fella's got to make a living,
all cathedrals, churches, chapels, and the parades
of gray habits, priests with guitars and school children
singing patriotic songs that swell the streets — I must let this be,
be something else, not Munich in 1933.
I forgive all tests of faith, all creeds,
but not the banishment of doubt.
I forgive not only because of my friends the Polish Poets —
they can do nothing if a man pumps gas
or a woman buys a blouse or returns it to the shelf.
I forgive, not for the Polish sun,
but for the earth that revolves around it.